OCT 13 2000

OCT 20 **Date Due**

NOV 29	NOV 1 2 1998
JAN 24	NOV 0 3 1999
APR 6	
MAR 1 1	DEC 2 0 2000
DEC 2 9 1983	FEB 1 2 2002
JAN 2 6 1988	MAY 1 0 2002
AUG 1 1 1988	
JAN 2 4 1992	
APR 0 7 1992	
SEP 2 2 1995	
JAN 2 9 1997	
JUL 1 6 1998	
SEP 1 5 1998	

CAT. NO. 23 233   PRINTED IN U.S.A.

131455

CANADA ON WHEELS

CANADA ON WHEELS

BY JOHN DE BONDT

A Portfolio of Early Canadian Cars

For Corrie

The automobile in Canada is older than Confederation. As early as 1851 Thomas Turnbull, a carpenter in Saint John, NB, built a three-wheeled wagon driven by what the Saint John *Weekly Chronicle* called "a crank of peculiar construction—the discovery of Mr. T—which is worked by two levers, one situated upon either side of the driver's seat." Somewhat indignantly the newspaper added that the "principal arrangements of this novel machine are in the body of the wagon, where they are covered and kept out of view . . . . Therefore it is impossible for us to pronounce from personal inspection of the machinery upon the value of Mr. T's discovery." Less reticent was Henry Seth Taylor, a watchmaker in Stanstead Plain (now Stanstead, Que.), who built a "steam pleasure carriage" in 1867. He told the Stanstead *Journal* that his car would run against "any trotting horse that can be produced" at the local fair and promised that it would "show some fast time." "This mechanical curiosity," the paper commented, "is the neatest thing of the kind yet invented." Fairgoers, however, failed to recognize Taylor's pioneer achievement and Canadians forgot about the whole thing until 1960, when the car itself was rediscovered. It has since been meticulously restored and is now on display in the Ontario Science Centre at Don Mills. Taylor's "mechanical curiosity" is not only the first self-propelled vehicle made in Canada but also one of the oldest in the world.

Canada's first gasoline-driven automobile was built thirty years later, in 1897, by George Foote Foss of Sherbrooke, Que. Two or three years later the first production cars were made by the Good brothers of Berlin (now Kitchener), Ont., who laid out a primitive assembly-line of 32 vehicles.

By that time, after 50 years of testing and experiment, the automobile was ready to take on the horse in a contest that was to change the face of Canada and the rest of the continent. The odds were heavily in favour of Ol' Dobbin: there were millions of horses in Canada, on the farms as well as in the cities. In Toronto, near the corner of Yonge and Bloor, Maher's Horse Exchange sold 600 to 700 horses a week at regular, twice-weekly auctions. That automakers were able to sell any cars at all is a wonder. Their early products were clumsy, hard to operate and totally unreliable. Roads, even in the towns, were abominable; there were no garages or service-stations; and mechanics were so unskilled that car-manufacturers warned against using them. Moreover, the shuddering, snorting machines frightened the horses. Early laws and editorials all reflect the country's genuine anxiety. In 1903, for example, Ontario speed-limits were set at a miserable seven miles an hour within 100 yards of any horse-drawn vehicle. The law also forbade motorists to drive "in a manner likely to frighten a horse"—at a penalty of $25 or 30 days in jail for first offenders. The Ontario Motor League went so far as to run "schools for restive horses" and in 1909 Prince Edward Island prohibited motor cars altogether. When, four years later, the island relaxed the rule and allowed cars on its roads three days out of seven, *Motor Age* explained that this would "allow horses to get used to cars."

Early motorists were despised by lawmakers, editors and farmers alike. In 1910, in the Ontario Legislature's Municipal Committee, Carleton MLA McElroy called car drivers "scoundrels" who "should be shot." ("But this excessive language met with disapproval from the committee," *Motoring* added.) In Newcastle, Ont. the *Independent* raged, "We can compare [motorists] to nothing but a lawless gang of hoodlums and stop they must . . . we must make an example of a few of them before a call to arms is given." The "example" took such drastic forms that the OML had to engage detectives to apprehend those who spread tacks or glass on the roads or strung wires across at neck-level, hoping to decapitate passengers in open cars.

Nevertheless, a growing number of Canadians not only bought and drove automobiles but built them too. Between 1900 and 1933 more than 125 different makes—not counting the numerous one-of-a-kind backyard experiments—were produced in Canada. Many were, of course, built by branch-plants of American automakers, but more than half were genuinely Canadian, in the sense that they were built nowhere else, at least not under the same name.

Within a few short years there had been two cars called the Canadian, as well as a Canada, a Canada Baby Car and at least one called the Dominion. There was a Regal and a Royal, a LeRoy, a Queen, an Earl and a Leader. There was the Iroquois and the Pontiac (still a popular car); there was an Arrow and a Dart, a Still and a Swift, a Comet and a Star.

As soon as cars were made in quantity for sale to the general public, automakers began to advertise them. From the outset the motor car has been a symbol of the good life for thousands of ordinary men and women, and for this reason early car ads like those in this collection offer a unique insight into the Canadian past, its likes and dislikes, its needs and desires, its hopes and fears. CCM, for example, urged readers to "get a Russell and enjoy our glorious open air and sunshine." Willys-Overland spoke of green meadows glinting with "mottled gold. Summer air stirs the fields of growing grain. All nature sets you yearning to drive this perfect summer car." Even Ford spoke of the "scent of growing things" and of butterflies dancing in the sun. For then as now car-makers—and their ad-men—were ready to offer the public, not just a car, but whatever it was they wanted, whether it was freedom or power, speed or beauty, convenience or comfort, dignity, grace or elegance.

The oldest Canadian company making cars today
is Ford, established at Walkerville
(now part of Windsor) in 1904.
The first Canadian Fords were assembled
from chassis and other parts
shipped by ferry, two or three at a time,
from Detroit. The bodies were made in Canada
by Wm. Gray & Sons of Chatham, Ont.
The first Ford plant at Walkerville was so primitive
it didn't even have electricity. The only piece of power equipment
was a drill, driven by a belt attached to the rear wheel
of one of the first cars made at the plant.
This is the 1905 Model C, of which 110 were built
at Walkerville the first year.
The two-cylinder car had a top speed of 30 MPH
and sold for $1100.

Just a year after Ford opened its first plant at Walkerville,
the Canada Cycle and Motor Company
(now better known for its CCM bicycles)
introduced the Russell.
CCM had already marketed an electric car,
the Ivanhoe, but in 1905 it switched
to gasoline engines.
The Russell, a two-cylinder car named after
the company's general manager, T. A. Russell,
soon established a reputation for high quality,
and for ten years CCM built a complete range of cars,
all "made up to a standard," as the company slogan said,
"not down to a price."
Early Russells didn't go very fast,
but those who wanted to know the exact speed
could buy a speedometer for $22.
Most owners settled for a less expensive status symbol:
their monogram on the doors for $3.
The car at right is the 1906 model.

The improbable scene at left was featured on the 1906 calendar
of the McLaughlin Carriage Company of Oshawa.
The elegant couple who have invested
in a McLaughlin Reliable Carriage (No. 165)
look with apparent indifference
at the terrible accident that has befallen
the motorists in the foreground.
The unlucky driver is forced to submit
to the attentions of a disapproving doctor,
immaculate in top hat and morning coat.
In 1906, when this ad appeared, McLaughlin was building
25,000 horsedrawn vehicles a year
and no doubt feared the challenge of the automobile.
Things changed quickly, however, and McLaughlin soon came to terms
with the new fashion.
The calendar for 1908 (below) shows a procession
of McLaughlin carriages and automobiles
out for a drive near Rouge Hill, east of Toronto.
McLaughlin built its first cars in 1908
and sold out to General Motors ten years later.

SATURDAY AFTERNOON

McLaughlin Carriages and Automobiles as seen on a
Saturday Afternoon, passing the "Rouge Hill," a popular
driveway 12 miles east of Toronto. An historic piece
of public highway on the old stage road between Toronto
and Montreal.

The Dominion, illustrated above, cost $1850 plus $130 for such optional extras as windshield, dustcover and mohair top. It had wheels with spokes of "second-growth hickory" and its makers claimed it delivered "a road speed of more than 50 miles an hour with a full load of passengers, with plenty of reserve power for climbing hills." The Dominion was introduced in 1910, first as the Dominion Thirty and later (perhaps because its four-cylinder motor produced at least 35 HP) as the Dominion Limited. Its makers stoutly claimed that it exploited "no freak or untried ideas."

One of the earliest Canadian car-makers was Tudhope-McIntyre of Orillia, Ont. The 1909 model at right had an imported McIntyre motor, reliable solid rubber tires and high wheels, essential on country roads. After a fire destroyed the plant in 1909, Tudhope started making Everitt cars, initially under that name, later under its own nameplate. The company switched to military production in 1914.

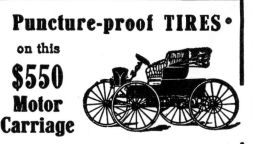

The Every Day Car,
like the Tudhope,
was a highwheeler
with solid rubber tires—
its chief claim to reliability
"every day in the year."
The Woodstock Automobile
Manufacturing Company
of Woodstock, Ont.
hastened to point out that
this was "a shaft-driven car—
not an automobile buggy."
It had no doors or windshield,
but came with lamps
and a top,
which in 1911 meant
it was "fully equipped."
The company also built
light delivery wagons
and four-passenger cars,
both selling for $750.

The "Every Day" Car
The Car for Service

CAN BE OPERATED EVERY DAY IN THE YEAR

No Tire Troubles

$ **650 Fully Equipped** $

6
5
0

6
5
0

THIS IS A SHAFT DRIVEN CAR—NOT AN AUTOMOBILE BUGGY

HE McLAUGHLIN ELECTRIC
= ON A RAUCH & LANG CHASSIS =

Electric automobiles were popular,
especially with women,
before the First World War.
Electrics often had front seats
that faced sideways
or backwards.
They were steered
from the back seat,
which allowed the driver
to sit "*with* instead of
in front of her friends."
McLaughlin marketed
this Rauch & Lang Electric
as the McLaughlin Electric in 1911.

COST OF OPERATING THREE ONE-HORSE VANS FOR FIVE YEARS		COST OF OPERATING ONE SCHACHT DELIVERY VAN FOR FIVE YEARS	
3 Vans at $250 each	$750	One Van	$2,150
7 Horses at $200 each	1,400	Gasoline at 60 miles per day, 300 days per year, 10 miles per gal.	1,440
3 Sets Harness at $40 per set	120	Oil at 50c per gal., 120 miles per gal.	375
Repairs to Harness at $5 per set per year	75	Grease, transmission and cup, at 15c per lb. running 100 miles to the lb.	135
Repairs to Vans, including repainting	525	Battery charging at 50c per month	30
Insurance at $25 per policy	375	Tire renewals at 5,000 miles per tire	3,300
Wages of three drivers at $15 per week	11,700	Oil for lamps	100
Wages of stablemen and general help (one at $10)	2,600	Repairs	375
Feed, stabling, vet service, shoeing, etc. at $25 per horse per month	4,500	Liability and fire insurance	750
		Driver at $15 per week	3,900
Depreciation at 20 per cent	1,870	Incidentals at $25 per year	125
Interest on investment at 6 per cent	480	Interest at 6 per cent	645
		Depreciation at 20 per cent	2,150
	$24,395		$15,475

Cost of operating three one-horse vans for five years	$24,395
Cost of operating one Schacht Delivery Van for five years	15,475
Saving in operating Van for five years	8,920
Net saving, per year, in favour of Schacht Delivery Van	$1,784

Schacht was a subsidiary of the Schacht Motor Car Company
of Cincinnati. It made both passenger cars
and delivery vans
at its Canadian plant.
This ad for the 1912 van
throws fresh light on life in early Canada.
Before World War I, for example,
horses cost $200
but drivers were worth only $15 a week,
$10 less than it took to keep a horse.
Tires were expected to last only 5000 miles
and cost $3300 in five years,
but the van itself was good for 90,000 miles
at a cost of only $375 for repairs.
It was the beginning of the end for the horsedrawn van.

Oldsmobile first established
a Canadian assembly plant
at St. Catharines, Ont.
in 1906 and two years later
opened a factory in Toronto.
Production was halted
before the War
but resumed in 1920
in the Oshawa works
of General Motors
of Canada.
The model at left
was built in 1910.
At the turn of the century
the Studebaker company
had been making carriages
for almost half a century.
The company made
its first car in 1902,
its last in 1966.
Canadian operations
started in 1909.
During the Twenties
the Studebaker sedan
was a favourite
with smugglers.
Even the 1912 model
shown below
was advertised as being
"faster than any car."

17

*"Made up to a Standard
—Not Down to a Price."*

Each part of a Russel car must pass through an Inspection Department where every man employed is paid to discover mistakes.

The Russell is the only car in Canada with the world-famous Knight motor. An interesting book will be sent upon request.

Write for the new catalog.

RUSSELL MOTOR CAR COMPANY, LIMITED, WEST TORONTO
MAKERS OF HIGH-GRADE AUTOMOBILES.

BRANCHES: Toronto   Montreal   Hamilton   Winnipeg   Calgary   Vancouver   Melbourne, Aust.

"*The Clinton is built by Canadians who know, for Canadians who can discriminate.*
In every essential it is just a little better than need be.
Durability, Reliability and Accessibility are the basic principles;
but attractive appearance and beauty of design have not been sacrificed."
"*The Brockville-Atlas, the advent of which has been so anxiously awaited*
by the automobile world, is now ready for the market.
It is the Car par excellence for Canadians. Built in Canada, by Canadians.
Designed especially for Canada
by men who with their unparalleled knowledge of conditions
have made it the ideal car for the discriminating buyer of moderate means
as well as for those who desire a Model-de-Luxe."

In 1909 CCM, makers of the Russell, obtained sole Canadian rights
to the Knight motor, a remarkably silent and durable
sleeve-valve engine hitherto used only on expensive European makes
like Daimler, Mercedes and Minerva.
The 1912 Russell-Knight limousine (overleaf, left)
was one of the most elegant cars ever made in Canada,
with its curved piping, bevelled glass, its flower vases and dainty coach lamps.
The 1912 Clinton (overleaf, top) featured a low running-board,
and was specially designed—or so its makers claimed—
to withstand the harsh Canadian climate.
The Brockville-Atlas (overleaf, bottom) was introduced in 1911.
This is the 1912 model.
A beautifully restored specimen of this rare car,
recently offered for sale for $25,000,
is now in the Canadian Automotive Museum at Oshawa.
Its body was built by the Canada Carriage Company
and it had a motor made by the Atlas Engine Works of Indianapolis.
The 1913 McKay (facing page) was one of the
few Canadian cars ever made in the Atlantic provinces.
The first McKay was built two years earlier
by the Nova Scotia Carriage Company at Kentville, NS.
Some two dozen cars were assembled there from American parts
and bodies made locally. Then in 1912
the Nova Scotia Carriage and Motor Car Company was formed at Amherst,
where another 150 McKays were built.
They were modelled on the Penn 30
and some, like the one shown here, had aluminium bodies.
The company went out of business during the First World War.

"McKAY"

An Announcement of Our 1913 Model

40 h.p. car with Mohair top, windshield, electric lighting system dynamo and storage, Truffault-Hartford shock absorbers, electric horn, Stewart speedometer, and full set tools.

    Seven passenger car with aluminum body - $2300.00
    Five Passenger - $2050.00   Roadster - $1950.00

30 h.p. car with Mohair top, windshield, speedometer, Truffault-Hartford shock absorbers, Presto tank, bulb horn, and full set tools.

    Five passenger touring car - $1585.00
    Roadster - - $1485.00

A truly high grade car, and one that will compete in every detail with the highest priced cars on the market. Specially designed for rough roads.

THE TALK OF THE MONTREAL SHOW
Catalogue for the Asking

The Nova Scotia Carriage and Motor Car Co., Ltd.

Office and Factory————————————AMHERST, N.S.

See This Car at the Exhibition
Compare It With Other Sixes

The difference in value in favor of this pioneer among high-class sixes can be seen at a glance. If you demand all the up-to-date features that are tried and proven—together with standard equipment unsurpassed by any other car—if price be a consideration with you—see this car.

When you have carefully compared cars, specification for specification; when you have compared prices, ask yourself this: "What dependable features have the more expensive sixes to offer which the Maritime-Singer has not got?"

Seven years ago the Palmer-Singer Mfg. Co., of New York, introduced the first successful six to sell for a comparative low price. No improvement is added until proven beyond doubt. The Maritime - Singer stands alone among sixes for big value. It is known as

THE STRONGEST CAR IN THE WORLD

It is strong. Finished up to the last minute in every detail of tried and proven construction, luxuriously comfortable, and handsome. At $3,000 no such car has ever been offered in Canada.

Some Specifications: New style body on handsome continental lines—50 horse-power—six cylinder—Westinghouse electrical starting and lighting system—128-inch wheel base—36 by 4½-inch tires—compressed air starter, with tire inflator ceptional—demountable rims—ball and roller bearings—Flaxon horn.

Price $3,000, F.O.B., St. John, N.B.
SEE EXHIBIT AT CANADIAN NATIONAL EXHIBITION.

The Maritime Motor Car Co., Limited
Rothesay Ave.   **St. John, N.B.**

The 1913 Maritime Singer Six (facing page) was the first
and only make of car built in New Brunswick.
Maritime was affiliated with the Palmer-Singer Company of New York,
which already had seven years' experience in building six-cylinder cars.
Unfortunately, however, the car cost far more to build than the $3000 it sold for
and production was stopped after only four or five cars had been finished.
The Maritime plant on the outskirts of Saint John
is used today by the New Brunswick Department of Public Works.
None of the Maritime Singers is known to have survived
and there are only the ads to tell us what they were like.

Feathered hats and figured dresses: these were the elegant days
of Canadian motoring on the eve of the First World War.
The 1914 Tate Electric (above) came as a roadster
and as a coupe, ideal for women "after five minutes' instruction."
The makers claimed that you could change batteries
"in about the same time as it takes to fill a gasoline tank."
Tates were built at Walkerville from 1913 until 1915.

The Last Chance

A limited number of "Galt" Motor Cars offered at a figure far below the cost of manufacture.

A wonderful opportunity to purchase a high-grade, electrically-equipped, roomy automobile. Read the specifications below, then write for the price—it will astonish you.

These cars must be sold at once.

Model "F" 14 Touring Car.

Specifications:

Horsepower—35.
Wheel Base—118 inches.
Cooling—Water, centrifugal pump.
Ignition—Generator, with storage battery and Connecticut distributor.
Lubrication—Combination force feed and gravity.
Clutch—Multiple disc, in oil.
Gear Ratio—4 to 1.

Tires—35 x 4'' Dunlop or Goodyear.
Front Axle—1 beam section, drop forging.
Rear Axle—Full floating.
Springs—Fowler, front, semi-elliptic rear, ¾ scroll, elliptic.
Wheels—Wood, artillery type, demountable rims.
Gasoline Capacity—15 gallons.

Color—Body, royal blue; chassis, black; enamel hood and fenders.
Equipment—Electric generator, storage battery, electric head, side and tail lamps, electric self-starter, electric horn, speedometer, windshield, top and envelope, power tire pump, full set of tools and repair kit. All nickel trimmings.

Write or Wire. CANADIAN MOTORS, LIMITED, GALT, ONT. Phone 443

The Galt was at first known
as the Canada Tourist and the Canada Roadster.
Built by Canadian Motors of Galt, Ont.,
it was renamed the Galt in 1911.
Its body was made of laminated poplar,
painted royal blue with "French grey" wheels.
Seats were upholstered
in hand-buffed black leather.
The touring car shown above was offered in 1914
as a "last chance" before the company went out of business.
It sported a bumper and a "power tire pump."

During the First World War prices came down
as skirts went up.
At $850 the 1916 Overland (below)
provided stiff competition
for the Model T Ford.
Willys-Overland,
named after John N. Willys,
founder of the parent company,
took over the old Russell plant
in West Toronto.
This was the beginning
of Kaiser-Jeep of Canada
(now part of American Motors),
which was formed in 1953
when Henry J. Kaiser bought Willys.
The first Willys-Overland cars
were made in Canada in 1914.
The name Overland was dropped in 1939.

The Maxwell, later advertised
as The Good Maxwell
and still later as The New Good Maxwell,
was the grandfather of the Plymouth.
First established in Canada before World War I,
the Maxwell Motor Company was later sold to Chrysler.
In 1925 Chrysler brought out a four-cylinder car
with a motor similar to that used in the Maxwell,
and in 1928 the four-cylinder Chrysler
was renamed Plymouth.
The 1917 model shown here
was built at Windsor
and cost $355 more than a Ford,
but it boasted an electric starter and lights,
a speedometer and gasoline gauge and came equipped
with tires good for up to 8000 miles.

M^c LAUGHLIN

Toronto University ~

THE new McLaughlin Master Six Roadster is the undisputed leader in the roadster class. The new radiator and hood and the unique body design of this model give it a racy appearance that is extremely pleasing. The smart, graceful lines, the speed, power and quick acceleration make it the favorite among men whose business demands the personal car.

Ladies who drive favor the roadster model of Canada's Standard Car because of its beauty, ease of control, its comfort, dependability and extreme roominess. Ample luggage space is provided by the large compartment in the rear. The driver of this McLaughlin Roadster is the discriminating motorist whose choice of a car is influenced by beauty and utility.

By 1921 McLaughlin cars had been on the road for almost fifteen years.
The 1921 Master Six Roadster (facing page)
sported a front bumper and a spare wheel rim,
but in spite of its "racy appearance"
only 1400 McLaughlins were sold that year.
Two years later the company sold over 17,000
McLaughlin-Buicks—more than in any other year until 1955.
The name McLaughlin-Buick came into use in the Twenties
and in time the McLaughlin name was dropped altogether.
Gray-Dort was owned jointly
by Wm. Gray Sons-Campbell of Chatham, carriage-makers,
and the Dort Motor Company of Detroit.
At one time the company had ten factories
and nearly 400 dealers across Canada
and between 1916 and 1924 built and sold more than 23,000 cars.
Dort failed in 1924 and the Canadian company closed the same year.
This is the 1920 model.

In its day the Chevrolet 490
was as famous as the Model T Ford.
It was introduced in 1916
and cost $490 in the United States
($130 more than the Model T).
The 1922 model (facing page)
is still called the 490,
despite the inflated price.
Early models carried an oil can under the hood,
since some parts had to be lubricated
by hand every hundred miles.

Chevrolet Model F, "Baby Grand"
Five Passenger Touring Car, $1225

Chevrolet Model F-A/2
"Royal Mail" Roadster, $1225

Chevrolet produced its first V-8 engine in 1917,
fifteen years before Ford.
Its makers claimed
that the new engine delivered power
"as constant as the flow of Niagara."
The new silhouette was long and low,
with a wheelbase of 120 inches,
and came in "lustrous Chevrolet green" only,
with a choice of several body styles
for two, four or five passengers.
McLaughlin obtained the Chevrolet franchise in 1915
and built the model illustrated above three years later.

"490 A" Five Passenger Touring
Car, $825

Chevrolet "490 A" Roadster,
$810

"490 A" Coupe, $1350

"490 A" Sedan, $1350

30

CHEVROLET

"490"

Thirty miles to the gallon is not unusual with the "Four-ninety." Oil consumption is very low—tire mileage very high.

"490" Touring $785

"490" Special $895

CHEVROLET "490"		CHEVROLET "F. B."	
Roadster	$785	Touring	$1,395
4-pass. Coupe	1,170	Special Touring	1,475
Sedan	1,195	Special Roadster	1,475
Light Delivery	785	Coupe or Sedan	2,195

All prices f.o.b. Oshawa—Sales Tax Extra

CHEVROLET MOTOR COMPANY
of Canada, Limited
Subsidiary of General Motors of Canada, Limited

OSHAWA   **WINNIPEG**

"490" Special

This is the 1922 Parker, a big, angular car
with a wheelbase of 127 inches,
a plywood body,
and a 70 HP Continental motor.
The Parker was one of a dozen or more
Canadian makes that have been built in Montreal.
The first Parker was finished in 1920
and a year later
the Parker Motor Car Company claimed
it had signed contracts for 3000 cars.
Like many other cars on the market in the Twenties,
the Parker was assembled from standard parts
made by firms specializing in certain components,
such as engines, frames,
axles or wheels.
The company failed in 1923.

The Tudor Sedan

Not even a chilly all-day rain need upset the plans of the woman who has a Ford closed car at her disposal. Knowing it to be reliable and comfortable in all weathers, she goes out whenever inclination suggests or duty dictates.

The car is so easy to drive that it constantly suggests thoughtful services to her friends. She can call for them without effort and share pleasantly their companionship.

All remark upon the graceful outward appearance of her car, its convenient and attractive interior, and its cosy comfort. And she prides herself upon having obtained so desirable a car for so low a price.

TUDOR SEDAN, $755   FORDOR SEDAN, $895   COUPE, $665   (All prices f.o.b. Ford, Ontario)

Though early Fords came only in black, the company was among the first
to advertise in colour. The charming ad for the 1924 Model T reproduced overleaf
was designed to appeal to women. At first Ford had adopted
a down-to-earth approach, announcing bluntly that the Model T
was "as easy to operate as a kitchen range." By 1924 the appeal is more subtle:
a closed car of her own gives a woman dignity, grace and independence—
all at a price her husband can afford to pay.
The 1926 Oakland roadster (above) was one of the most dashing cars
on the road in its day, with its rumble seat and locker for golf clubs.
The first Oakland was made in 1908 but it wasn't until 1922
that production started in Canada. By that time Oakland was
part of General Motors and four years later the company introduced a new line,
Pontiac, Chief of the Sixes. Pontiac outsold Oakland from the start
and in 1930 the Oakland discontinued production in Canada.

SPECIAL DODGE BROTHERS MOTOR CARS IN FOUR TYPES

Four special types have recently been added to Dodge Brothers standard line of motor cars—

A Touring Car, a Roadster, a Type-A Sedan, and a 4-Passenger Coupe.

These types have been created for that substantial group of motorists who favor individuality in motor car appointment and design.

In fundamental construction they are identical with Dodge Brothers standard product. Their accentuated smartness however, is strikingly obvious in many elaborations of equipment and refinements of detail.

Special 6-ply, balloon-type tires, nickel-trimmed radiator shell on touring car and roadster (optional on closed types) front and rear bumpers, motometer with lock, special blue leather upholstery (for touring car and roadster) special body striping, rear view mirror, automatic windshield wiper, scuff plates, cowl lights and steel disc wheels constitute the more important items of special equipment.

DODGE BROTHERS MOTOR COMPANY
LIMITED
WALKERVILLE, ONTARIO

The Dodge brothers, who until then
had been working for Ford,
brought out their first car in 1914,
but it wasn't until 1924
that the first Dodge (overleaf) was made in Canada.
It had a four-cylinder motor,
replaced by a six
four years later
when the company was absorbed by Chrysler.
Note that the ad features such items
as a rearview mirror
and a windshield wiper
as "special equipment."
Cadillacs were built in Canada from 1923 until 1936.
The 1927 coupe below, with its elegant landau irons
(actually the car was a hardtop)
and characteristic double beltline,
was a luxurious car.
The 1924 Ford sedan illustrated opposite sold for $895,
more than twice as much as the cheapest Model T,
and the ads were designed accordingly, in delicate colours,
to appeal to men and women of taste and means.
The section of Windsor where the Ford plant was situated
was known as Ford, Ont. from 1913 until 1929.

CADILLAC
STANDARD COUPE

36

Its ability to contribute to the daily life of her children, as well as to her own, is a feature the modern mother is quick to appreciate in the Ford Four-door Sedan.

It opens to her a precious participation in their busy affairs. With a Ford Closed Car she can share their good times and yet hold to the necessary schedule of her day. She finds in it the qualities she desires most, and at a price extremely low in comparison with its high value. She enjoys driving it herself; and the children look forward eagerly to their rides with mother at the wheel.

Ford
CLOSED CARS

BROOKS STEAMER

the gentle giant of motion

The generating of STEAM POWER in a BROOKS STEAMER through making steam from water in a boiler over a kerosene or gasoline burner is a motionless process, which means NO MOVING PARTS are involved in it. It takes place entirely independent of the engine, making possible the STORING OF POWER over and above normal requirements for use when additional power is necessary. This power is CONTROLLED BY THROTTLE ONLY, and, being independent of the engine, devices such as gear shift and clutch are eliminated. The power is applied to the rear axle through the engine, which is instantaneously responsive to the change of steam admitted to it by the throttle, and the entire range of power from zero to the very maximum can be applied to the rear axle in an instant without even interrupting the flow of power, by merely sweeping through the full motion of the throttle lever, resulting in POWER CORRECTLY GENERATED, POWER CORRECTLY CONTROLLED AND APPLIED.

Brooks Steam Motors, Ltd.

(Toronto Branch)

King and York Sts.   **Tel. Elgin 5815.**

Plant:
Stratford, Ontario.

Factory Branches:
Toronto, Montreal, Ottawa.

The Brooks Steamer was the last
wholly Canadian car built by an independent maker.
Introduced in 1923, it came in a single model
and sold for $3600 and up.
By 1926, when this ad appeared,
Brooks Steam Motors of Stratford, Ont.
were still producing only a car a day,
and the next year the company closed for good.
Only about 170 Brooks Steamers were finished. A number
were used as taxis in Stratford, Toronto and Ottawa.
The 1927 Willys Great Six (below), a big, powerful, virile-looking car,
was driven by a Knight sleeve-valve engine like the earlier Russell.
Note that the headlights, cowl lights and fog lamp
all match the sculptured radiator shell.
The last Willys-Knight was made in 1932 but many are still in use.

Few illustrations could speak more eloquently
of the tone and style of the late Twenties
than the full-page ad for the 1927 Hupmobile
reproduced opposite:
the fashionable women,
with their short skirts,
bobbed hair
and boyish figures,
and the luxurious motor car,
with its drum headlights,
overhanging roof
and double beltline.
The Hupp Motor Car Company was established at Windsor in 1910
and for more than a quarter of a century
the name stood for high quality,
advanced styling
and good taste.
The company never recovered from the Great Depression
and went out of business during the Second World War.

Beauty, Color Options, Luxury in
ten enclosed and open bodies

The straight-eight is the ultimate motor principle.
Hupmobile is its finest expression. The combination means
that there literally is nothing more distinguished in motoring

IN THE FINE CAR FIELD, THE TREND IS UNDOUBTEDLY TOWARD EIGHTS

THE DISTINGUISHED
HUPMOBILE
EIGHT

In December 1928 Chevrolet announced
"A Six at the Price of a Four,"
a tremendous scoop.
Ford stayed with its four-cylinder Model A
for another three years
and Plymouth switched only in 1933.
The new Chevrolet (below) was the first of a long line
of six-cylinder Chevies
that eventually replaced Ford
as the world's largest-selling make.
"By every standard of comparison,"
one contemporary ad proclaimed,
"the outstanding Chevrolet of Chevrolet history."
The 1929 Dodge (facing page, top)
was the first Dodge car
produced under Chrysler ownership
and already there are touches of Chrysler styling
in the radiator, headlights and hood louvres.
The name Dodge Brothers was kept for many years
because, as the company explained,
many buyers chose the car
on "the sole recommendation of its name."

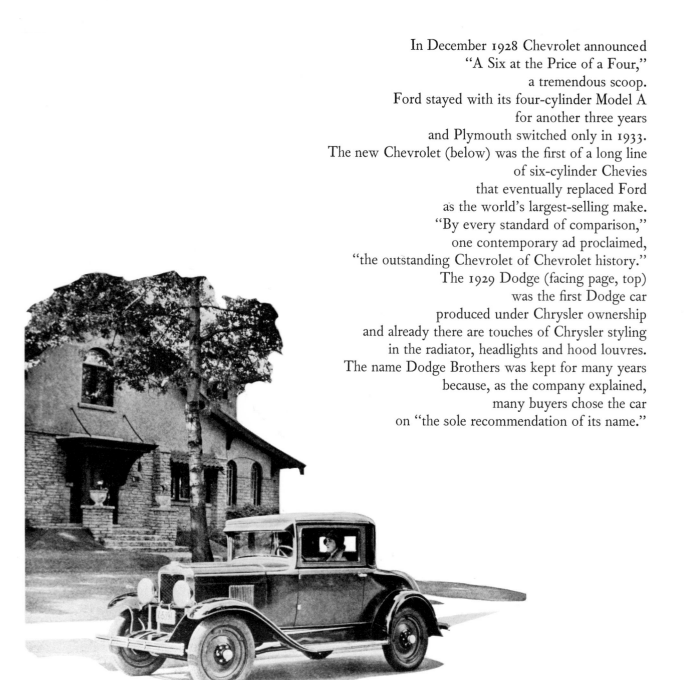

42

The first Plymouth was the 1929 model (facing page, bottom).
Successor to the four-cylinder Chrysler
and Chrysler's answer to the Model A Ford,
the new make established itself at once as one of the Big Three.
At a starting price of $850,
if offered such luxuries as side-valves
and four-wheel brakes.
Early Plymouths shared with other Chrysler cars
a number of delicate styling features
nearly lost to the modern eye,
such as the gentle curves that show
on windows, windshield pillars and hood louvres.

Ye Powder
Horn

CHRYSLER
PLYMOUTH

The Hudson was a forerunner
of the American Motors cars of today.
American Motors of Canada,
like its American parent,
was born in 1954
from a marriage of Nash and Hudson.
Hudson opened its first Canadian plant
at Tilbury, Ont. in 1931.
This is the first Canadian Hudson.
Its wire wheels,
side-mounted spare wheel,
box trunk,
chrome trim and landau irons
made this one of the most impressive cars on the market.
Added features were an adjustable steering-wheel
and adjustable front and back seats.

The Model A Ford succeeded the Model T in 1928.
A quarter of a million were built in Canada between 1928 and 1932
and thousands are still on the road.
One of the rarest and most desirable today
is the pretty 1931 two-door deluxe phaeton
shown here parked on the sunny main street
of a small Canadian town forty years ago.

The last of the Canadian cars was the Frontenac (below).
It was made by Dominion Motors of Toronto,
who also held the Durant franchise in Canada.
The Frontenac was introduced in 1931
and lasted for just two years.
It had an American-built motor
and came in four- and six-cylinder models.
The major American automakers had had branch-plants in Canada
since the earliest days of motoring in this country,
but since the middle Thirties
all so-called Canadian cars have been built in a few main centres—
such as Oshawa for General Motors, Windsor for Chrysler
and Oakville for Ford—
by branch-plants of the great American corporations.
Canadian cars no longer have a distinctive identity
and the colourful and evocative story
of Canadian car-makers and their cars
has long since come to an end.

The *Frontenac Six*

A Canadian Built Car

NOUVEAU
PONTIAC SIX

ROULEMENT LIBRE
DEUXIEME SILENCIEUSE
EMPATTEMENT PLUS LONG

NOUVELLES
CARROSSERIES FISHER
CONFORT DE ROULEMENT
RESSORTS COUVERTS
CONTROLE DE SOUPLESSE
AUGMENTATION DE
PUISSANCE

CHEF DES VALEURS

Library of Congress Card No. 76–122317
ISBN 0 88750 021 8

Many people in all parts of Canada have helped in the preparation of this book. The author is particularly grateful to John W. Anderson, Gordon E. Armstrong, Bob Belier, Wilf Bell, Bert Bentley, Léon Brassard, Herb J. Brennen, Gilbert Bureau, George Burgess, Lorne C. Callbeck, Mary M. Cattie, Patricia Curran, Earl B. Davison, Mrs. Hugh C. Elliott, Ron Fawcett, Fred Ford, Dorothy Foss, William Murray Gray, Madeleine Grenier, R. O. Harrison, Mrs. J. L. Harvey, W. G. Heaman, John Howard, J. Hurdis, Sandy Intini, Mrs. H. H. Jacobs, A. W. James, Neil A. Matheson, Wm. H. McCurdy, Robert S. McKay, Ian McNab, Bill C. Meacher, D. G. Minnes, K. A. Narraway, Gordon Neale, Bud Oatman, Jean-Marie Paradis, Wm. A. Parker, George H. Peckover, Rick Percy, Chas. W. Proctor, Sherwin Raichman, Lucide Rioux, Glen Robinson, G. P. Rogers, Charles Roy, William Sauder, Art Shearer, George Shepherd, C. Grant Slinn, Gordon E. Smith, Herman L. Smith, Rae Smith, Shath Square, M. W. Stahl, A. Stranges, Alan Suddon, F. Thompson Jr., George Turner, Colin P. Vezina, Wallace Ward, Peter A. B. Weather-head, Charlie Weaver, Floyd Westling, W. P. Young. The advertisements for the 1912 Russell, the 1927 Cadillac and the 1927 Willys-Knight are from the G. Andrew Burgess Collection. The advertisements on pages 4, 14 (top), 15 (bottom), 17 (bottom), 22, 23, 24, 32, 38 and 46 are from the Toronto *Globe* (22 April 1922, 19 July 1910, 1 September 1911, 29 August 1912, 2 September 1913, 19 November 1913, 11 April 1914, 22 April 1922, 20 April 1926 and 9 September 1931); those on pages 9, 11, 16, 18, 19 (top), 25, 28 and 45 are from the *Canadian Magazine* (April 1905, July 1906, May 1912, February 1912, April 1912, June 1916, May 1921 and May 1931); those on pages 29, 31, 33, 35 and 43 are from *Maclean's Magazine* (1 June 1920, 15 May 1922, 15 March 1924, 15 April 1924, 15 June 1929 and 15 August 1928); those on pages 27 and 30 are from the *Farmer's Magazine* (11 June 1917 and 15 February 1918); those on pages 36, 39 and 42 are from *Canadian Homes and Gardens* (November 1926, September 1927 and July 1929); those on pages 15 (top) and 19 (bottom) are from *Rod and Gun in Canada* (August 1911 and March 1912); those on pages 12 and 13 are from the McLaughlin Carriage Company Calendars for 1906 and 1908; those on pages 6, 14 (bottom), 17 (top), 21, 34, 37, 41, 44 and 47 are from *History of the Queen's Own Rifles* (1901), *Canadian Courier* (27 March 1909), *American Magazine* (March 1910), *Motor Magazine* (1913), *Saturday Evening Post* (15 May 1926), *Canadian Home Journal* (February 1924), *Vogue* (15 March 1927), *Good Housekeeping* (February 1931) and *La revue moderne* (February 1932).

Book designed by Michael Macklem

PUBLISHED IN CANADA BY OBERON PRESS

PRINTED AND BOUND IN ENGLAND BY BERIC PRESS LIMITED
AND HAZELL WATSON AND VINEY LIMITED